T0128376

This Side of Glory
and other poems

D. E. MINES

WESTBOW
PRESS®
A DIVISION OF THOMAS NELSON
& ZONDERVAN

WestBow Press books may be ordered through booksellers or by contacting:

WestBow Press
A Division of Thomas Nelson & Zondervan
1663 Liberty Drive
Bloomington, IN 47403
www.westbowpress.com
1 (866) 928-1240

Scripture taken from the New King James Version®. Copyright ©
1982 by Thomas Nelson. Used by permission. All rights reserved.

ISBN: 978-1-9736-7874-8 (sc)
ISBN: 978-1-9736-7873-1 (e)

Print information available on the last page.

WestBow Press rev. date: 12/03/2019

To my wife
and children
for the joy they bring to living

Preface

Why write a book when there are so many already? Strange as it may be, even in this digital age some people would rather hold a book in their hands than stare at a computer screen. I'm one of those. Maybe you are too. My interaction with a writer through the printed page in my hand doesn't depend on having an electrical source or internet connection. O course, there are advantages to having an entire library of down loaded e-books stored on a portable drive that's not much larger than a deck of cards. But still, I read only one book at a time.

As a child my favorite companions were books. My parents were convinced that I would rather read than eat. I spent many hours solving mysteries with the Hardy Boys as well as with Nancy Drew. I took my sword and sailed into battle against the French with Captain Horatio Hornblower or experienced the outer limits of time and space guided by Ray Bradbury or Isaac Asimov. Books gave me a picture window view of wonders and a doorway to countless delights and discoveries. They still do.

Growing up I often fantasized about becoming a writer. So it seemed natural for me to do a book like this. The impulse for poetry came from my paternal grandmother, Sam. Sam was grandad's affectionate term for grandmother Sarah, who was herself a prolific writer of verse. My preacher father was also greatly involved in communicating through the printed page. Now that I have retired I have an opportunity to turn a childhood fantasy into rewarding reality.

This book gathers together a number of my poetic thoughts written at different times and under various circumstances throughout the years, thoughts about significant moments in life. and meaningful personal relationships. The poems are not arranged in chronological order but loosely grouped around three general themes. Along the way there have been those who heard or read these lines and found them meaningful and moving. My hope is that you will be among that number. To God be the glory.

Round Rock
2019

I
The Journey

Micah 6:8
He has shown you, O man, what is good; and what
does the Lord require of you but to do justly, to love
mercy, and to walk humbly with your God?

John 8:12
The Jesus spoke to them again, saying, "I am the
light of the world. He who follows me shall not
walk in darkness but have the light of life."

On This Side of Glory

On this side of glory
We sometimes journey through deep shadows
Until the sunshine breaks through.

We have not journeyed alone.
Others have traveled with us and
They are part of our story.

At times they walked behind us
Supporting us with their prayers.
At times they walked besides us
To share some burden that weighed us down.
At times they walked ahead of us
To pave the way,
      To set a course
           Or lead by example.
Their laughter lifted our spirits.
Their songs stirred our souls.
Their courage challenged our commitment.

They grace our lives
By the gift of who they were and
How they lived
On this side of glory.

Now their voices echo
In the chambers of our memories.
Though they've reached home before us,
We thank God they blessed us all
Still on this side of glory.

Launch Out

It's best for men, amid the streams of life,
Not to flounder in the shallow pools,
but venture forth, invade the deep, where strife
does flow and fashion stouter souls of fools.

Mistress

The sea is amorous
and only by her permissive calm
do ships caress
her lacy bosom
and only on unworthy lovers
does her feverish tempo rail.

Through Barren Lands

Beyond the silent, shifting sands
the weary pilgrims rest.
Their wanderings through these barren lands
your comradeship has blest.

Though Paths Do Part

Though now our paths appear to part,
allow not strangeness in between,
nor time permit to rob your heart
of friendship for a friend unseen.

About it All

Why is life so complicated
work so hard, and joys belated?
Why am I so irritated
about it all?
Why must things be so debated
till the issues are misstated
and often chaos is created
about it all?
Yet life is not so complicated
and you alone are not frustrated
for others too are aggravated
about it all.
So to the haste be acclimated,
you yourself accelerated.
You needn't be infuriated
about it all.
So when trials seem accentuated
and conflicts more accumulated
let your hope be activated
about it all.

A Night in Waiting

I wait
and the thousand eyes of night
look down on me and cry,
but I can neither feel their tears,
nor can I touch the sky.
I wait
and the thousand eyes of night
look down on me and weep,
but I can neither soothe their sorrow
nor can I sleep.
I wait
and the thousand eyes of night
look down on me and say
"Be patient, weary child of night,
Twill soon be day."
And so
I wait.

The Dreamer

I count my dreams by all the stars above
and whisper to the breeze when one doth fall.
I search the night for friendship and for love
and sleep when only dawn has heard my call.
O'er silent sands I walk a lonely shore,
the sea's breast heaving chants, the sighing wings,
all cry together, "Dreamer, dream no more
but spend your days in doing all those things
of which you dream and birth your dreams at will.
With hands yet strive to catch that falling star".
But then the siren call of wind and sea grow still
and somewhere in the mist beyond the bar
as all the stars are swallowed by the dawn,
my heart stands quiet and silently dreams on.

The Wall

Somewhere
between two silent hearts
there stands a wall too firm
for words to breach, too broad
for thoughts to span.
It soars
far past the point of hope
to some far distant height
beyond my reach and strength
to understand.

When Love Seems Lost

When dim the vision grows
of youth's romantic dreams,
and love is plagued by hordes
on one's own selfish schemes,
when anger steals the joys
of golden moments shared,
and each believes the other
may have ceased to care,
when faults appear more real
than virtues hidden deep,
and love once vitally alive
seems dead in endless sleep,
In heartache let trust break through
and God will true love renew.

One Brief Encounter

One brief encounter, you and I,
and suddenly all time is now,
for both the past and future die
and to this hour no bounds endow.

A Pure Embrace

Love is as delicate as lace
and woven of the simplest strands,
the tenderness of a pure embrace
and a heart that understands.

The Walk

We simply walked the trails that day.
For goodness knows how long,
But as we shared the scenic way
My heart was filled with song.

We strolled beneath the flaming spires
And found an altar crest,
Where, as we shared the evening fires
My soul found peace and rest.

To sit with you beside the stream
Was joy indeed for me,
And as we shared some humble dream
You made all sorrows flee.

No matter where our pathway led
I found the way complete.
And even when no word was said
I found each moment sweet.

My Traveling Prayer

When I am gone
Let people say
It was a joy
He passed this way.
I hope it's true
That where I go
Some worthy gift
I can bestow.
A bit of song
To cheer the day,
A helpful thought
To guide one's way.
A newfound friend
Forevermore,
A little poem
Tacked on the door.
Through every day
Both foul and fair,
This is, O Lord,
My traveling prayer.

II
The Growing

2 Corinthians 3:18
"But we all, with unveiled face, beholding as in a mirror,
the glory of the Lord, are being transformed into the same
image from glory to glory, just as by the Spirit of the Lord."

John 16:33
"These things I have spoken to you, that in Me you
may have peace. In the world you will have tribulation;
but be of good cheer; I have overcome the world."

I Corinthians 10:13
God is faithful, who will not allow you to be tempted
beyond what you are able, but with the temptation will also
make the way of escape, that you may be able to bear it.

On Barefoot Days

On barefoot days of boyhood
I'd stroll a path of damp packed sand
between the dunes and sea
and play a game of catch-me-if-you-can
in my world of salty air and sun
I'd wade in seaward to
test the depths with care
Then quickly dance away as breakers take up the chase
lest underhanded currents capture me
and pull me down for good
to end my barefoot fun.

The Better Poet

I did not write a poem today.
There really wasn't time
to think of something good to say
and put it into rhyme.

I was too busy sensing things
of beauty all around;
the melody the forest sings,
the flowing water's sound.

I read the lines that God did write
in trees and flowers and sky,
the poetry of seasons and of light
God's a better poet than I.

The Boy I Admire

He's only a boy in a newspaper hat
    but he marched at my side
    with a grown-up stride
and I had to admire him for that.
His warm little hand was swallowed in mine
    and with eyes straight ahead
    hardly a word would be said
as we marched down the line.
We strolled between the trees that bordered our road
    and I saw in his eye
    while marching on by
his mind must be carrying a man-size load.
He's big for his age though just only four
    but I'm sure he has grown
    much more than is shown
by the marks on the dining room door.
Though only a boy in a newspaper hat
    his thoughts reach high
    when he looks to the sky
and I have to admire him for that.

The Kite Flyers

Just a boy and his dad
with a bright yellow kite
on a good steady breeze
soaring over the trees.
The wind caught the laughter
of their afternoon's joy,
those moments of pleasure
for a dad and his boy.
with a smile and a shout
they played out their twine
and coached their kite higher
'till they had no more line.
The yellow kite flew
like a bird on the wing,
the wind playing music
on the pressure tight string.
But soon it was down
and folded away.
Yet restless to fly once again
on some other day.
You might say it was only
a cheap plastic toy.
but it made that day special
for a dad and his boy.

While Daddy is Away

Well, daddy has to travel.
I'll be gone for several days.
Of course you know I'll miss you
No matter where I stay.
So this is just to tell you
that even while I roam
my heart is thinking of you
though I can't be at home.
I know you will be helpful
to mommy every day,
to keep our home a happy place
while daddy is away.
Those little things that you can do,
like putting toys away
will keep a smile on every face
while daddy is away.
I also hope you'll not forget,
when you and mother pray,
that God is watching over us
while daddy is away.
So be your best at home and school
then all of you can truly say
"I'm glad that no one misbehaved
while daddy was away."
And when my traveling work is done
I will come home to stay.
The days, though long, will seem but few
that daddy was away.

My Heart an Echo Hears

Yes, I've noticed that you've grown.
Seeing you in that long dress,
the one your mother with much love has sewn,
just means I didn't really guess
the years had flown away so fast.
Of course, you're right
We can't hold back the years
to try and make your childhood last
But still, when late at night
I take a last quick look 'fore turning in
it's then my heart an echo hears
of yesterday's laughter when you were small
and sitting on my knee.
Yes, I've noticed that you've grown.
No doubt it's just my age and not your own
that puts me in this mood
to dream about the child that's gone
and wonder 'bout the woman that is to be.
I guess the thing that really bothers me
is how birthdays come on roller skates
to catch us by surprise.
It is so sudden, or so it seems,
you've turned fifteen and face your becoming years.
I can see the gleam that's in your eyes
is but your star of hope, your guiding light of dreams.
Yes, I see how much you've grown,
and all my hopes for your tomorrows
are bright in the promise of the girl you are today.

For Wounded Lambs

An ancient wise man wrote,
"a brother's born of adversity,"
And it was so, when sudden agony
Took hold of us and smote
Our hearts with pain too great
To bear alone, that he was there,
And, like the strong and gentle shepherd
That he serves, to care
For wounded lambs.

He shared the weight
Of sorrow life had brought our way,
And out of his own healing let us see
How truly adequate God's grace can be
when, to the strong and gentle shepherd
that he serves, we come
As wounded lambs.

In the Quiet of the Night

In the quiet of the night
beneath a mountain moon
a dreamer sought his heart song
but woke without the tune.
With the coming of the light
at the dawning of the day
he woke to nature's music
to cheer him on the way.

That Quiet Grace

There is a place by waters still
And while the hours pass
Between the golden edge of dawn
And the falling curtains of the night,
Your soul can find that quiet grace
Where you can wrap yourself in silence
And hear the voice of God.

Be Still!

Lord, what can I say
when I'm too tired to think,
and have no strength to pray?
Before we talk
could I but rest awhile?
that always seems to help.
No doubt you too have had a busy day
listening to countless urgent pleas
So Lord, for now,
it is enough that you are here
And I'll just sit and listen.

Along the Way

We've covered many a mile, my dear.
We've travelled to and froe.
We've watched it rain a while, my dear
.and huddled in the snow.
We've climbed the hill and crossed the glen.
And every place we've been
Was a lovely place to know.
Was a lovely place to know.

We've dreamed with starlight in our eyes
And watched the moon take flight
We've waited for the sun to rise
And burn away the night
We've listen to the season's song
And every trail we've walked along
Was a lovely way to go, my dear
Was a lovely way to go.

We've gathered flowers along the way
And chased the rainbow's end
We've laughed with children at their play
And chatted with a friend
We've known the day to go too fast
But every happy hour we've passed
Was a lovely time to live, my dear
Was a lovely time to live.

Amid These Hills

Amid these hills
Where often we have stood before
To count together the passing of the years,
and mark our memories
With celebrations and with tears,
We've come once more
To where our hearts can hear
The lingering whispers of past farewells.
How good to have these friends still near
At hand
amid these hills.

Amid these hills
We've shared in days both dark and bright
And, sharing, forged a bond made doubly strong
That still holds firm to our delight,
And gives us hope to sing through future years
The song we learned to sing as one
Amid these hills.

Amid these hills
You leave behind a legacy of work well done
And host of friends who wish you well
As on you go to other joyous tasks not yet begun.
So come what may, these simple lines are meant to say
You're always in our hearts
Amid these hills.

Ebenezer

Through all the past our God has led
To bring us to this day.
So for our future let us vow
To trust His guiding way.

III
The Hope

2 Corinthians 4:17
For our light affliction, which is but for a moment,
is working for us a far more exceeding and eternal
weight of glory, while we do not look at the things
that are seen, but at the things which are not seen.

I John 3:2
Beloved, now we are children of God; and it has not yet
been revealed what se shall be, but we know that when He is
revealed, we shall be like Him, for we shall see Him as He is.

Voices Out of Darkness

They were voices out of darkness,
Deep and hard,
Yet singing of the light
And hope.
They were voices rising through despair
To lift the spirit's song of freedom.
They were voices dark and deep,
Conceived within demeaning depths
That rose up out of inner earth
To shape their songs
In the crucible of time
And give to hope new birth.

To Think on Greater Things

I long to sit by a quiet sea
and watch the sun go down
while stretched out wings go soaring free
away from the salt laced ground.
So may my spirit seek its flight
and seek what lies beyond my view;
to think awhile on greater things
and come away with mind renewed.
I'd make the shore my kneeling place,
the song of the sea my prayer,
and seeing stars in heaven's face
to know that God was there.

Credo

I believe.
I believe that I am
I exist and this is where my creed begins.
Yet in my heart
I know that I'm not the beginning.
I am face to face
with marvels and mystery
and wonderments that have no ends.

I stand beneath a star filled sky
and wonder not how, but why
this world and all that is has come to be?
Before there were beginnings
and not a single star to see,
nor was there me
Some have said that God thundered into emptiness
a shout of creative power
So there was light and water,
earth and flower
All of it was good and needed care
so God made someone with whom to share
since loneliness is not a good so
God made you and me

Crossroad Moments

Reunions are full of crossroad moments
when paths we've followed meet once more
and, for a while, we pause to reconnect
and shape a mosaic of different memories.
The stories of our many journeys
are woven together as a tapestry
of witness to the grace of God.

My Bamboo Garden

1

To walk in the sun
when the day comes blowing cold
gives a man new strength

2

that moment of fear
in the midst of our striving
should make our faith strong.

3

Night rides the cold wind
to chase the winter sun while
waiting for the spring.

4

When two hearts are one
life's every joy is doubled
and burdens made less.

5.

Late is the night hour
when one puts away his work
if day was well spent.

6.

A thousand mirrors
reflect my garden's roses
once the rain has gone.

7.

Each wave that comes in
washes out to sea our fun
in sand castle dreams.

8.

A lover's pathway
is laid across the water
by a peeking moon

9

Songs of traveling wings
heard beneath a pale, grey moon
tell us winter comes.

10

A little boy's song
brings a gentle peacefulness
to his father's heart.

11

A daughter's bright smile
fills her father with singing
on a cloudy day.

The Stammering Candle

The stammering candle in the night,
that whispered its last breath,
lay conquered by the wind of fright,
the dark its gown of death.

The Lesson of the Night

On heaven's velvet cloak inscribed
one finds this lesson of the night;
as deeper grow the shadows black
the stars give greater light.

The Song that has no Ending

For us, his voice is silent,
the light of his eye is gone,
and though we walk toward evening
he's already reached the dawn.
He woke up in the morning singing
where aging takes no toll,
for the song that has no ending
was the music of his soul.
He took his melodies for living
from the score of the Sacred Word,
and stayed in tune by heeding
the sweetest song he'd heard.
Within our hearts we hear him.
His voice rings clear and strong.
"I'll sing of the lovingkindness
of the Lord forever,"
as one of heaven's throng.
Let not our voice be silent
though our eyes be dim with tear
While still we walk toward evening
let all around us hear,
that in God's forever morning,
in the light of eternal day,
He's still alive and singing
where dying has no role
for the song that has no ending
is the music of his soul.

Printed in the United States
By Bookmasters